S0-CMR-405

Selections from

EDVARD GRIEG

Lyric Pieces

Piano Solos by Master Composers of the Period

Edited by Dale Tucker

CONTENTS

Editor: Dale Tucker
Art Design: Joann Carrera
Artwork Reproduced on Cover: *Il Segnale* by Daniel Ridgeway Knight

EDVARD GRIEG
Born: June 15, 1843-Bergen, Norway
Died: September 4, 1907-Bergen, Norway

Edvard Grieg was born to musical parents in Norway on June 15, 1843. His father played the piano moderately well, but his mother was considered a gifted pianist and singer who had performed with orchestras in their city of Bergen. She was Edvard's first music teacher, and from her he developed his intense love for music. Grieg had a great interest in poetry as a boy and often spoke of being a poet or a minister when he grew up. He was not considered a good student, academically or musically, as he was lazy about his studies and practice schedule.

Grieg began composing as a young boy, but his compositions were not taken seriously until he was in his early teen years. A visit to the Grieg home by noted violinist and composer, Ole Bull, exposed the first recognition of Grieg's true talent. Bull saw and heard some of 15-year old Edvard's compositions, and persuaded his parents to send him to the Leipzig Conservatory. There, his health suffered and took him away from his studies for a time, but he returned, winning honors in composition and piano until he graduated in 1862.

As a composer, Grieg often felt uninspired, and considered himself unsuccessful. However he began to write music inspired by his native Norway, giving the world insight into this lovely country and its people. This proved to be a positive avenue for him, although it was some time before works were performed and he was accepted as a noted musician. Among those who appreciated his writing was Franz Liszt, and also a cousin, whom he later married, who was a singer. For her he composed many songs.

In general his piano works are not difficult, his songs are lovely and reflective of his native land, and his orchestral works are still often performed today. He also became a successful orchestra conductor, and toured Europe in this position. Grieg was awarded many honors during his life, including honorary Doctorates from Cambridge and Oxford Universities.

Grieg suffered a heart attack in early September, 1907 and died only two days later. As a final honor, his body lay in state following his death, and thousands came to pay a final tribute.

ARIETTA

Opus 12, No. 1

EDVARD GRIEG

Poco andante e sostenuto

WALTZ IN A MINOR

Opus 12, No. 2

Allegro moderato

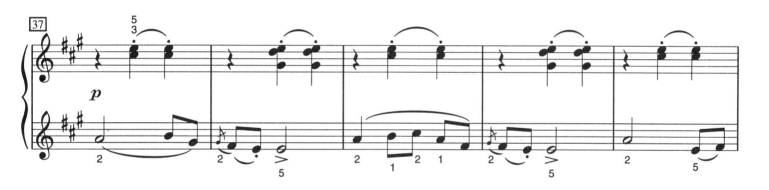

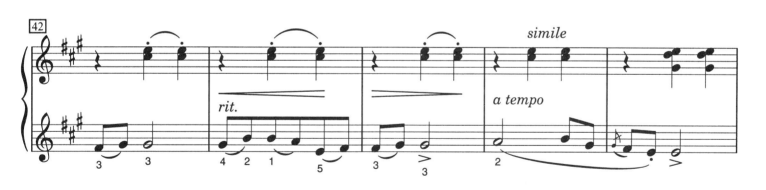

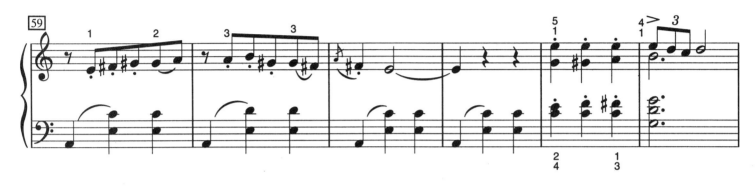

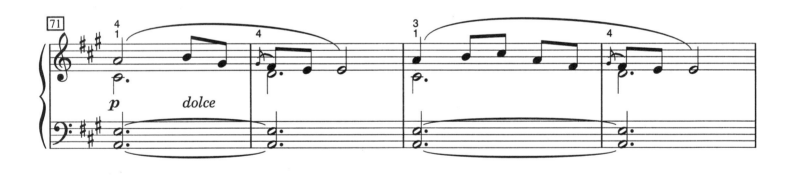

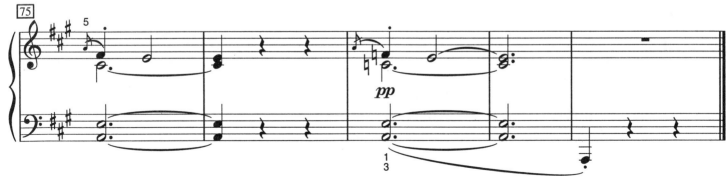

WATCHMAN'S SONG

Opus 12, No. 3

Molto andante e semplice

ELF DANCE

Opus 12, No. 4

Molto allegro e sempre staccato

ELM00039

NATIONAL SONG

Opus 12, No. 8

POPULAR MELODY

Opus 38, No. 2

Allegro con moto

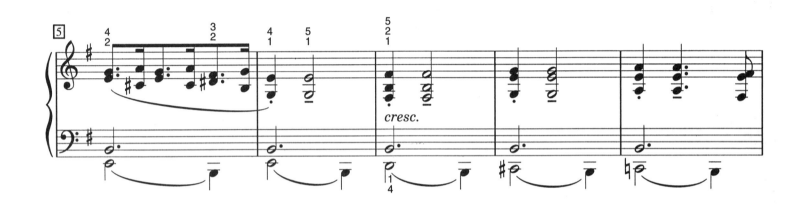

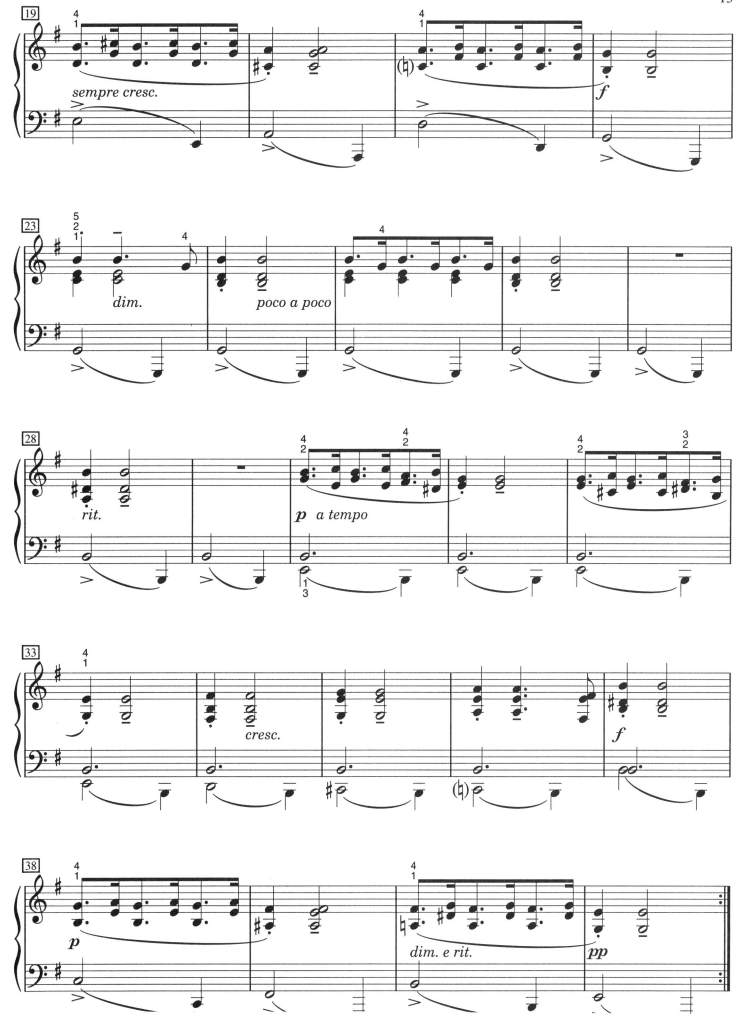

SPRING DANCE

Opus 38, No. 5

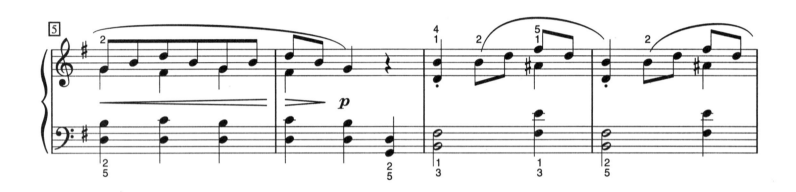

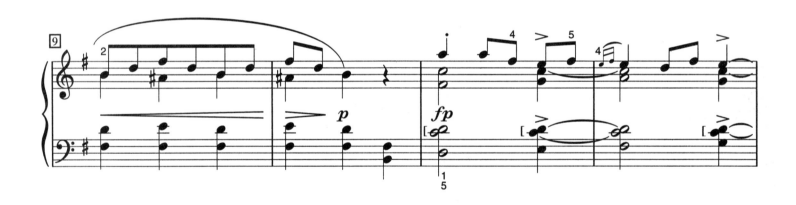

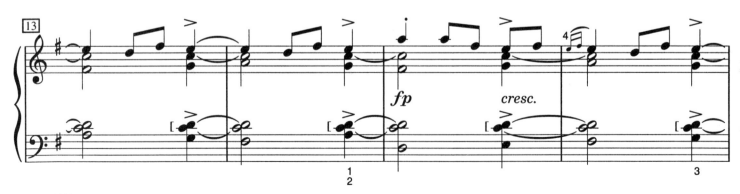

WALTZ

Opus 38, No. 7

Tempo I

Lento

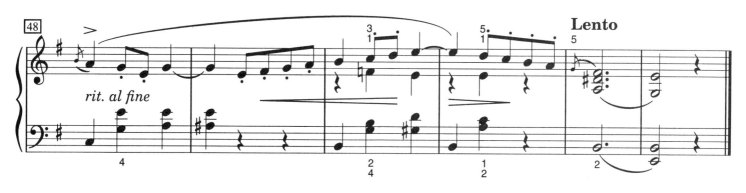

MARCH OF THE DWARFS

Opus 54, No. 3

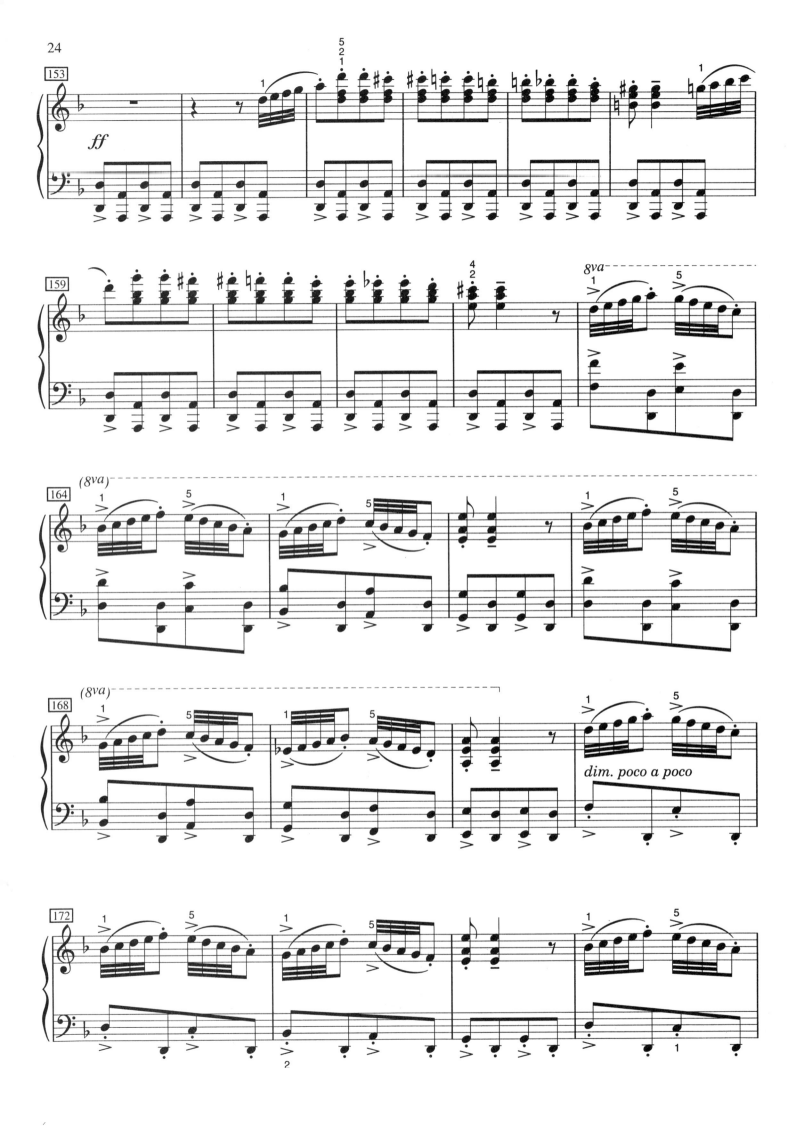

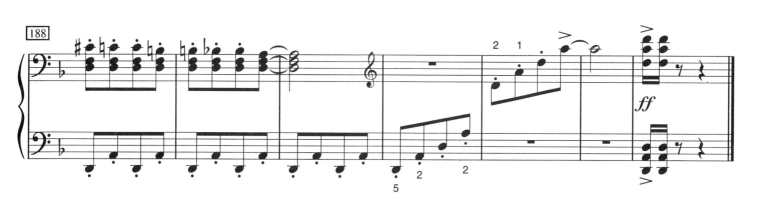

NOCTURNE

Opus 54, No. 4

SAILOR'S SONG

Opus 68, No. 1

Allegro vivace e marcato

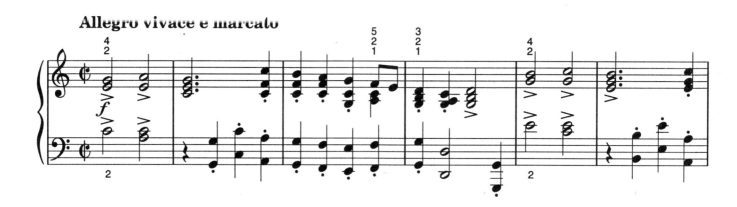

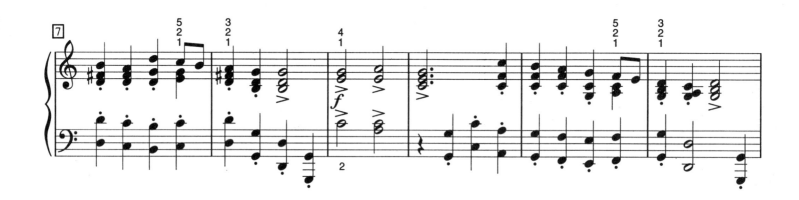

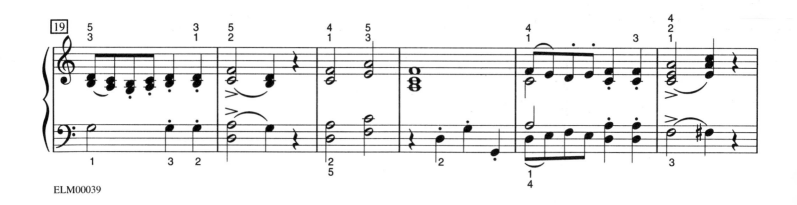

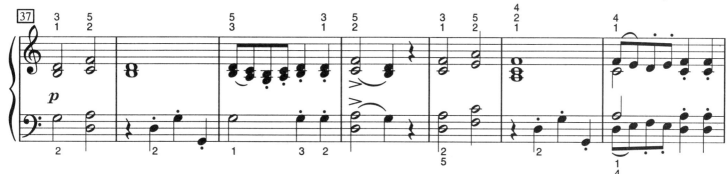

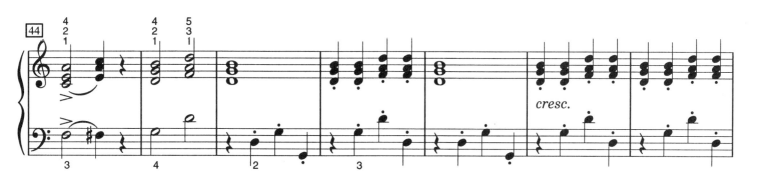

ELM00039

GRANDMOTHER'S MINUET

Opus 68, No. 2

Allegretto grazioso e leggierissimo

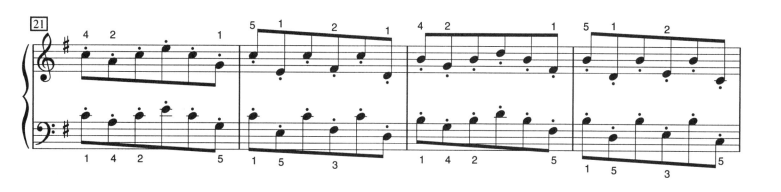

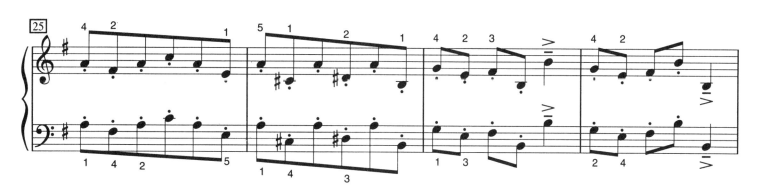

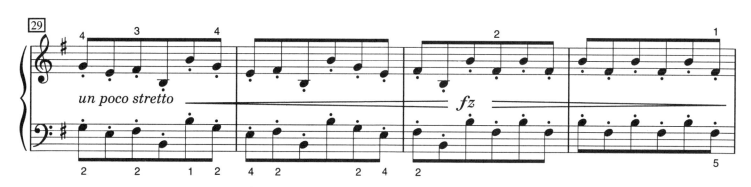

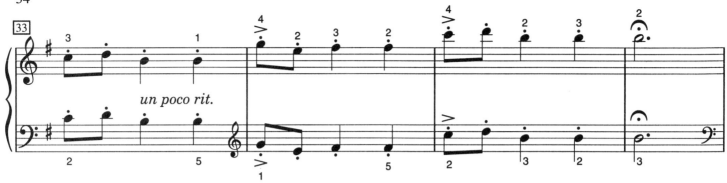

Tempo I

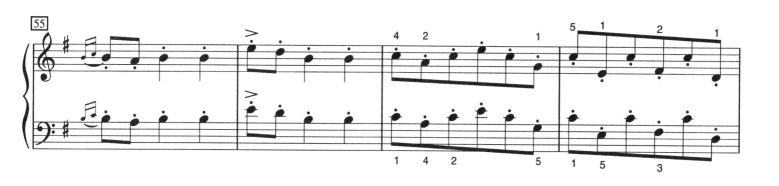

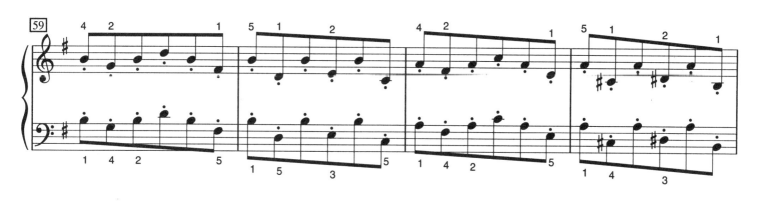

ELM00039

PUCK
Opus 71, No. 3

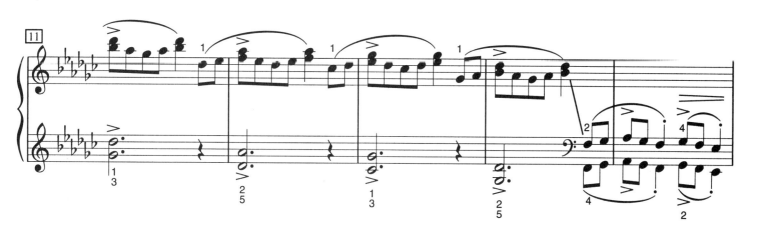

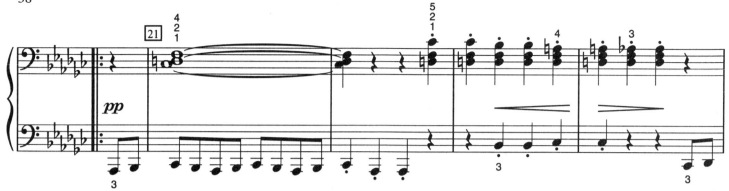

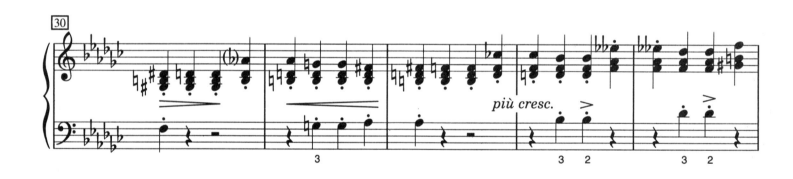

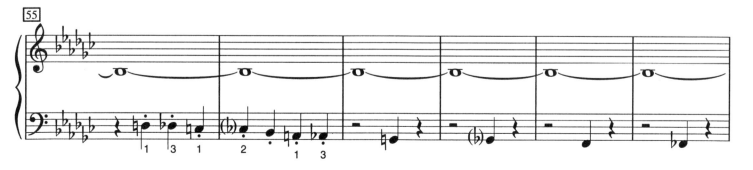

REMEMBRANCES

Opus 71, No. 7

Tempo di valse

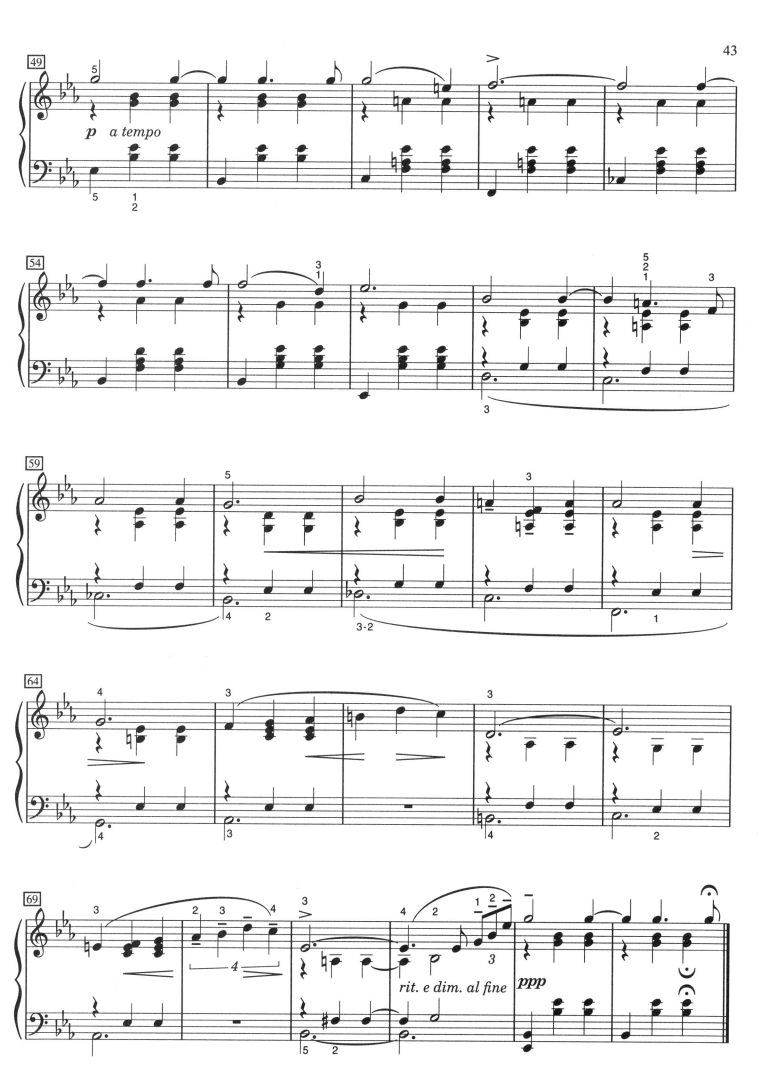